Make It Happen!

Wé McDonald

SINGER

BY RYAN HUME

Lightswitch
LEARNING

150 East 52nd Street, Suite 32002
New York, NY 10022
www.lightswitchlearning.com

Educators and Librarians, for a variety of teaching resources, visit www.lightswitchlearning.com

Library of Congress Cataloging-in-Publication Data is available upon request.
Library of Congress Catalog Card Number pending

ISBN: 978-1-68265-574-0
ISBN: 1-68265-574-1

Wé McDonald by Ryan Hume

Edited by Lauren Dupuis-Perez
Book design by Sara Radka
The text of this book is set in Neuton Regular.

Printed in China

Image Credits

Cover: Newscom, Jackie Brown
Page 1: See credits for cover
Page 4: Getty Images, iStockphoto
Page 5: (top) McDonald Family Archive; (middle) Getty Images, John Sciulli; (bottom) McDonald Family Archive
Page 6: McDonald Family Archive
Page 7: Getty Images, Fotosearch RF
Page 8: Kimeth McClelland
Page 10: Getty Images
Page 11: Getty Images
Page 12: Steve Schnur
Page 14: McDonald Family Archive
Page 15: McDonald Family Archive
Page 16: Steve Schnur
Page 18: McDonald Family Archive
Page 19: McDonald Family Archive
Page 20: Getty Images, Gary Gershoff
Page 21: Getty Images
Page 22: Getty Images, John Sciulli
Page 23: McDonald Family Archive
Page 24: Jase Michael

"Success is when you enter this world and make a beautifully large impact."

WÉ McDONALD

• • •

Make It! HAPPEN!

Before Reading

Think about your own goals.
Do you want to play soccer or write stories or make music? All of these activities take time and practice.

During Reading

During reading, keep an eye out for the highlighted vocab words. While learning about Wé's story, pay attention to how she got to where she is today. What **skills** has she shown that have helped her **career**? In each chapter, the Make It Happen! activity will help you, too, build skills to reach your own goals.

After Reading

Look in the back of the book for questions and activities to help you think about Wé's story.
Share these with a friend, parent, or teacher. Also, talk about the skills you need to reach your goals.

skill: the ability to do something that comes from training, experience, or practice
career: a job or profession that someone does for a long time

Contents

Even at six years old, Wé was showing interest in music.

Standing on a stage and singing to judges is a challenge most people do not face. For Wé (sounds like "way") McDonald, it's just another step in her journey.

Wé became famous on *The Voice* in 2016. *The Voice* is a television show. Singers compete for the chance to make music. Wé did not win, but she finished in third place. She is an **innovative** jazz and pop singer. Today, at 18 years old, she has entertained millions with her amazing voice. But first, she had to overcome **bullying**, both at school and at the start of her career.

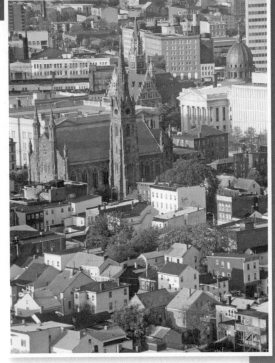

Wé was born in New York City, but she grew up in Paterson, New Jersey.

innovative: having new ideas about how something can be done
bully: to frighten, hurt or threaten someone

Wé was born in New York City. She first lived in the neighborhood of Harlem. It has a history of jazz music. Jazz musicians use pianos, guitars, trumpets, saxophones, and other instruments. Wé listens to jazz. It inspires her to make her own music style.

Wé's sisters and her brother all love music. They are her biggest fans.

Her Own Sound

Wé's family inspired her to be a singer. Her mom and grandparents are singers. Her sisters also sing. There was always music playing in their home. A lot of times, her dad played jazz.

Wé's mom introduced her to soul music. Just like jazz, soul is an important part of African American history. "I don't want just to be able to do soul," Wé said in a YouTube video. "I do listen to a lot of hip hop [and] pop, actually. I listen to a lot of country [and] a lot of **alternative** stuff. I feel like it gives me a new **perspective** on stuff." Listening to a lot of different music can help singers find their own sound.

Wé also listened to Michael Jackson. His blend of soul and pop music inspired her. His success influenced her career goals, too. "If I'm a quarter of what Michael Jackson was, I've succeeded so much," she told the magazine *Teen Vogue*.

alternative: not usual or traditional
perspective: a way of thinking about and understanding an issue

Make It! HAPPEN!

Explore Your Interests

Turning something you love to do into a career can be a great idea. Do you love to sing, like Wé? Maybe you love to write stories or play video games? Here's what you can do to begin to plan for an innovative and fascinating career:

- Search for a career with your interest in mind. Online, try searching for "Jobs for ___." Put your interest in the blank space.
- What type of jobs came up? Make a list.
- Search for jobs with another interest you may have. Are the results similar?

Share your job list with a parent or teacher. Together, you can make a plan to turn what you love into a possible future career.

First Steps of the Journey

The Apollo Theater opened in 1913. The theater can hold more than 1,500 people.

Ever since she was a little girl, Wé has been involved with music and the arts. "I don't remember not loving the arts," she said. "That was always something that I loved to do. When I was 6, I started playing piano. I started dancing at 11. And I was 12 when I realized that I could sing and that I could actually make a career out of that.'"

New York City is famous for its innovative theater and music.

Wé liked to sing along with her older sisters. They would perform in front of their family, often singing at family barbeques. Wé would also watch her sisters perform at school talent shows and knew she wanted to sing, too. She started singing lessons at 11 years old. Her dad suggested that she enroll in an after-school program. This gave her more time to practice and taught her **self-direction**.

self-direction: the ability to organize and guide yourself

Taking the Stage

All of this hard work landed Wé on stage at just 16. **Amateur** Night at New York City's Apollo Theater is famous for its crowd. The audience is encouraged to "boo" people off the stage. It's a tradition, which means it's how things have always been done.

Wé was scared when she heard about the tradition. In the theater, there is a tree stump called "the tree of hope." People rub it for luck. Wé gave it a rub and went on stage.

Wé had to get through many **tryouts** before taking the stage at the Apollo Theater.

amateur: a person who does a sport or hobby for pleasure and not as a job
tryout: a test of someone's ability to do something that is used to see if he or she should join a team, perform in a play, etc.

"The first thing I thought going out on stage was, 'I hope that I kill this,' and then I blanked out," she recalled. "I barely remember what the **performance** was like. All I remember was my family screaming and me crying at the end. And then I saw the audience [score], and I got like a 95 [out of 100]."

performance: an activity that a person or group does to entertain an audience

By facing her fears and singing her heart out, she made it through—and finished in first place that night.

Make It!
HAPPEN! Speak to a Group

Speaking in front of a group of people is an important skill. You will need to be confident and **flexible**. Public speaking often happens in school and at work.

flexible: willing to change or to try different things

- Write an essay about a time when you were speaking or performing in front of a group of people.
- How did you prepare? Were you nervous? Did your hands sweat? Did your voice shake?
- If you love performing and speaking in front of an audience, explore why that might be.

Why do you think it is important to learn to speak in front of others? In what ways can you improve?

Overcoming Obstacles

In middle school, Wé worked hard to make friends. This included joining sports teams.

In sixth grade, Wé moved to a new school, far away from her friends. Almost right away, Wé was **bullied**. She was shoved and called mean names. Bullying is not always physical. A lot of bullying involves name-calling, making up rumors, or leaving people out. Her parents went to her teachers and the principal, but nothing happened. The bullying continued.

Wé's family tried to help her while she was being bullied. She felt stronger with their support.

obstacle: something that makes it difficult to achieve a goal
resilience: the ability to become strong, healthy, or successful again after something bad happens

Wé was lonely. She was bullied by her classmates during sixth, seventh, and eighth grade. "There must be something wrong with me," she thought.

Her father, Mac, told *Essence* magazine that Wé did not want to leave the school, saying, "She wanted to hold on and fight and challenge all of her **obstacles**." By doing this, Wé grew strong. This **resilience** prepared her to sing in front of large crowds.

Bullying Beyond School

By the time she started high school, Wé was focused on her acting, singing, and dancing. Wé made new goals in the arts. She also took the **initiative** to make sure she reached her goals. Reaching these goals made her a stronger person. When asked what she would tell other kids who are being bullied, she said, "Be strong. These people aren't going to mean anything to you [after high school]. I promise."

Bullying does not just happen in school. For Wé, one of the hardest things about working in the music **industry** is how much people focus on looks. Industry people can be rude or mean sometimes.

Wé didn't let bullying stop her from starting a successful career in music.

initiative: the determination to learn new things on your own; the ability to get things done
industry: a group of businesses that provide a particular product or service

Wé has faced a number of rude people as she follows her dream. People have told her to change her voice and that her hair is too big. "When they look at me, they think that I have to be a Rihanna or a Beyoncé," she said, "I will sing and I will say what I want to say." Wé has developed strong **self-esteem**.

self-esteem: a feeling of having respect for yourself and your abilities

Make It! HAPPEN! Discover the Music Industry

There are many jobs in the music industry, both on stage and off. Many require **leadership** and other useful skills. Even if you don't sing or play an instrument, you can have an exciting career.

What do you need to start? What skills do you need to succeed? How much money would you make? These are all important questions to ask. Take some time to learn about the jobs below.

leadership: the power or ability to guide other people

- Music producer
- Recording engineer
- DJ
- Music journalist

Pick your favorite job in the music industry. How can you prepare now for that career?

Teamwork

Wé's singing coach, Ms. Yolanda Wyns, helps train Wé's voice for big events, like singing the national anthem.

We's family has been there for every step along her journey. Wé's father is also her **manager**. Wé has described her dad as very strict and serious. "He kind of trains me like how you would train an athlete," she said.

Wé's family joins her before every audition to help keep the jitters away.

In fact, her dad surprised her with *The Voice* **audition**. Wé was already a fan of the show. On *The Voice*, judges don't look at a person until after they sing. Wé said, "Coming from my past, I thought, 'They don't know what you look like. They just go off what they're hearing.' And I think that's the most fair thing."

On audition day, her family kept Wé in a good mood. Her dad gave her advice. He told her to stay focused. Her mom said she loved her, while her sister just said, "Don't mess up."

manager: someone who directs the professional career of an entertainer or athlete
audition: a short performance to show the talents of an artist

What Love Sounds Like

Two of Wé's teachers have also had a big impact. One, Mr. Smith, was strict. But he taught Wé and her classmates "to reach past our **potential** in whatever we were doing in life," Wé said. "He embraced the weird in everyone. Because, after all, if you're an artist, you're **top-tier** weird."

Wé's singing coach, Ms. Yolanda Wyns, taught her that **"insecurities** shouldn't be holding me back." Instead, insecurities should be "building on the emotion of how I sing. And [I should be] defeating them with my success."

Alicia Keys became another important mentor for Wé.

potential: an ability that someone has that can be developed to help that person become successful
top-tier: at the highest level in a group, organization, etc.
insecurity: the feeling of not being confident about yourself or your ability to do things well

Then, Wé met the famous musician Alicia Keys. She was Wé's coach on *The Voice*. Keys told her, "I don't want to be like anybody else. And I don't want you to be like anybody else. You were born to show people what love sounds like." Wé and Keys worked well together. They picked and practiced songs for Wé to sing on the show.

Make It! HAPPEN!

Audition for the Arts

Auditions are a good way to showcase your talents and **creativity**.

- Find an event with open auditions. It might be a play, musical, band, or dance group.
- Get familiar with what you are auditioning for. For example, read the play or watch the musical.
- Practice by yourself and with a friend or family member.
- Before the audition, take care of yourself by getting a good night's rest and eating a healthy breakfast.

Did you succeed at the audition? If not, you can ask the judges what you can do to improve. Keep working on building your skills. Then try again at the next audition.

creativity: the ability to make new things or think of new ideas

Since being on *The Voice*, Wé has become well known. She has been invited to sing at many important events.

Even before *The Voice*, Wé was working on taking the music world by storm. In 2015, Wé won a music **scholarship**. She was chosen from around 700 other high school students from New York. The scholarship enables students to learn how to make hit **records**. It also shows them the money side of the music business.

By the age of 17, Wé started college. She is the only student at her college working toward a degree in jazz singing. This shows she has good self-direction. It lets her continue improving her singing skills while getting an education.

On *The Voice*, Wé did not win the grand prize. She finished in third place. "I was actually relieved," Wé said. "I knew I was in the Top Four. I was going to be fine. I couldn't have been happier just to be there at that point."

For Wé, *The Voice* was the first step toward a big career. She is happy about her time on the show, but wants to keep moving forward.

scholarship: money given to a student by a school or organization to help pay for the student's education
record: music put onto a CD or computer; to put music onto a CD or computer so that it can be heard later

Wé keeps improving her singing skills. She is working hard to reach more fans.

A Busy Life

Even though she did not win, Wé's experience on *The Voice* changed her life. It has led to many new opportunities. After the show, Wé's performances were put on CDs and online. Wé has also hit the top of the iTunes chart a number of times.

Now, she says, "My life is beautifully **hectic**." Wé continues to balance school, vocal practice, and performances all around the nation. In January 2017, she put out her own song, "Wishes." She has plans to release many more songs.

hectic: very busy and filled with activity

"Success is when you enter this world and make a beautifully large impact, and leave a **legacy** behind," Wé said. "That doesn't necessarily mean that you have to be a president, a CEO, or a superstar. That means that wherever your world is [...] you should leave an impact there and help change a life at a time, even if it's only one."

legacy: something important handed down from the past

Make It! HAPPEN! Record a Demo

To introduce yourself to record companies, you will want to take the initiative and record a "demo." A demo is a recording of one to three of your best songs. Follow these steps to make your first demo.

- Start your band. This can just be you, or include friends and family.
- Write your songs. Use inspiration from events in your life.
- Put the songs to music. You can play an instrument or use a computer program.
- Practice your songs until you think they are perfect. Play them for other people who can give you advice on how to make them better.
- Use a computer to record your demo.

How did it turn out? How can you improve on your next demo?

Defining Moments

Wé started singing and acting at the age of four. She has had many important moments in her career.

2009

Wé moves to a new school and is bullied by others. She works hard and refuses to let other kids hurt her.

2012

In the eighth grade, Wé joins an after-school arts program. There, she practices her singing and gets to perform. She also makes new friends.

2015

Wé takes the stage at Amateur Night at the Apollo Theater. She overcomes her fear of the crowd and finishes in first place.

2015

Wé wins an important music scholarship. She learns about how the music industry works.

2016

Wé joins *The Voice*. She makes it into the Top Four and finishes in third place. She sings her own song, "Wishes," for her final performance.

2017

Wé receives the Harlem Stage 2017 Emerging Artist Award.

Depth of Knowledge

1 What does it mean to "leave a legacy behind"?

2 Summarize the ways in which joining the after-school arts program helped Wé.

3 How have Wé's resilience, self-esteem, and self-direction helped her become successful?

4 Write a guide for how to get onto a talent show like *The Voice*. What steps can someone take? What skills are needed and why?

5 What is your opinion on the best way to overcome bullying? Write about the best way to handle bullying. Support your point of view with facts from the story.

Organize a Talent Show

In a group of at least six people, make your own talent show like *The Voice*.

STEPS TO TAKE

1 Design your talent show. Make notes on what it will be about. Will it have people sing, dance, or do other talents? Be sure to come up with a name for your show as well.

2 Discuss each member's talent and compare it to Wé's. Choose who will be judges and who will be contestants.

3 Set up a space for your show. You will need a stage and a place for the judges to sit and watch.

4 Have each contestant perform, with the judges providing advice.

5 Once you are done, talk about the show and how it went. Do any group members want a career in the music industry? What can they do now to prepare? For help, use Wé's story and the work you have done in the Make It Happen! sections of this book.

Glossary

alternative *(noun)* not usual or traditional (pg. 8)

amateur *(noun)* a person who does a sport or hobby for pleasure and not as a job (pg. 12)

audition *(noun)* a short performance to show the talents of an artist (pg. 19)

bully *(verb)* to frighten, hurt or threaten someone (pg. 7)

career *(noun)* a job that someone does for a long time (pg. 4)

creativity *(noun)* the ability to make new things or think of new ideas (pg. 21)

flexible *(adjective)* willing to change or to try different things (pg. 13)

hectic *(adjective)* very busy and filled with activity (pg. 24)

industry *(noun)* a group of businesses that provide a particular product or service (pg. 16)

initiative *(noun)* the determination to learn new things on your own; the ability to get things done (pg. 16)

innovative *(adjective)* having new ideas about how something can be done (pg. 7)

insecurity *(noun)* the feeling of not being confident about yourself or your ability to do things well (pg. 20)

leadership *(noun)* the power or ability to guide other people (pg. 17)

legacy *(noun)* something important handed down from the past (pg. 25)

manager *(noun)* someone who directs the professional career of an entertainer or athlete (pg. 19)

obstacle *(noun)* something that makes it difficult to achieve a goal (pg. 15)

performance *(noun)* an activity that a person or group does to entertain an audience (pg. 13)

perspective *(noun)* a way of thinking about and understanding an issue (pg. 8)

potential *(noun)* an ability that someone has that can be developed to help that person become successful (pg. 20)

record *(noun)* sounds, music, or images put onto a CD or computer (pg. 23); *(verb)* to store sounds, music, or images on a CD or computer so they can be heard or seen later (pg. 25)

resilience *(noun)* the ability to become strong, healthy, or successful again after something bad happens (pg. 15)

scholarship *(noun)* money given to a student by a school or organization to help pay for the student's education (pg. 23)

self-direction *(noun)* the ability to organize and guide yourself (pg. 11)

self-esteem *(noun)* a feeling of having respect for yourself and your abilities (pg. 17)

skill *(noun)* the ability to do something that comes from training, experience, or practice (pg. 4)

top-tier *(adjective)* at the highest level in a group, organization, etc. (pg. 20)

tryout *(noun)* a test of someone's ability to do something that is used to see if he or she should join a team, perform in a play, etc. (pg. 12)

Read More

Brière-Haquet, Alice. *Nina: Jazz Legend and Civil-Rights Activist Nina Simone.* Watertown, Mass.: Charlesbridge, 2017.

Etingoff, Kim. *Bully on Campus & Online.* Broomall, Pa.: Mason Crest, 2014.

Frankel, Erin. *Weird!: A Story About Dealing with Bullying in Schools.* Minneapolis, Minn.: Free Spirit Publishing, 2012.

The Giant Book of Children's Vocal Solos: 76 Selections from Musicals, Movies, Folksongs, Novelty Songs, and Popular Standards. Milwaukee, Wis.: Hal Leonard Corp., 2016.

Kaplan, Arie. *American Pop: Hit Makers, Superstars, and Dance Revolutionaries.* Minneapolis, Minn.: Twenty-First Century Books, 2013.

Robertson, Robbie. *Legends, Icons, and Rebels: Music That Changed the World.* Toronto, Ontario: Tundra Books, 2013.

Internet Links

http://www.nbc.com/the-voice

http://money.howstuffworks.com/how-to-become-a-singer.htm

http://www.joy2learn.org/jazz/

http://www.voicescienceworks.org/voice-science-for-kids.html

https://www.stopbullying.gov/kids/index.html

https://pacerkidsagainstbullying.org/

Bibliography

FRP TV. "Wé McDonald talks about performing and songs her father used to play in the house." *YouTube*. YouTube, 13 Oct. 2016. Web. 06 July 2017.

NBC The Voice. "The Voice 2016 Blind Audition - Wé McDonald: 'Feeling Good.'" *YouTube*. YouTube, 20 Sept. 2016. Web. 10 July 2017.

Weingarten, Christopher R. "Amateur Night at the Apollo: Behind the Boos." *Rolling Stone*. Rolling Stone, 11 Mar. 2015. Web. 19 June 2017.

Wiest, Brianna. "'The Voice' Singer Wé McDonald on Alicia Keys and Her Music Idols." *Teen Vogue*. TeenVogue.com, 25 May 2017. Web. 19 June 2017.

Wills, Cheryl. "Meet 'The Voice' Contestant Wé McDonald." *Essence*. Essence.com, 25 Oct. 2016. Web. 06 July 2017.

Index